Introduction

Any honest inquiry into the Primal Instincts of humanity will necessarily lead to a clearer understanding of their nature, their functions, and their potentialities, and so will help to pave the way for the appearance of a healthier and happier race of men. The dictum "Learn to know yourself," inscribed on the Temple of Apollo at Delphi, has never been of more vital importance, both individually and nationally, than it is to-day, and the various schools of modern psychological thought, which are steadily opening up those hitherto scarcely explored regions whence flow the springs of human actions, are gradually clearing away the ignorance which has been the real cause of so much disease and distress. The following chapters are to be welcomed particularly as an effort at the constructional reform of our treatment of one of our deepest and most powerful instincts. Even those who do not necessarily give assent to all the details in the line of argument therein pursued must surely approve the insistence upon the vital necessity of there being love in all sex relationships.

The word "sexual," though indispensable perhaps in such a book as this, invariably induces some measure of opposition by reason of the associations which it calls up, and so is often replaced by the cognate adjective "racial," which emphasizes the wider aims of Race Preservation rather than the narrower matter of the reproduction of individuals. It is not a matter of curing individual immorality, not even of explaining it only, it is the greater matter of laying a sound foundation for a practicable social morality that is the object of consideration here. It is important that any such opposition should be neither hypocritical nor hyper-critical, for great national issues are at stake. Without the healthy mind there can be no healthy body, at any rate from the point of view of the community, and thus such a scientific inquiry as is set forth in these pages is definitely leading towards the production of a healthier nation.

The necessity of there being established a balance between an unlimited self-expression and a rigid self-repression is clearly indicated also, and the importance of self-control is not ignored here as it has been elsewhere, unfortunately, both as regards the individual's physical health and the weal of the community at large; for self-control is a vital essential in the health of a man just as it is a vital necessity for the continuance of a nation. The following pages contain information and suggestions which should tend to the formation of a wiser and more hopeful outlook over the problems of sexual morality, and should therefore receive the careful consideration of all who have the interests of humanity at heart.

F. W. W. GRIFFIN
M.A., M.D., M.R.C.S., L.R.C.P.

March 1922

Contents

CHAPTER
1. APOLOGIA
2. OFFICIAL ATTITUDES TOWARDS SEX
3. THE GENERAL PRINCIPLES OF PURITY
4. CELIBACY
5. NON-CELIBACY
6. DIVORCE
7. EUGENICS AND PROSTITUTION
8. THE HOMOSEXUAL TEMPERAMENT
9. THE SEXLESS CLASS
10. SUPER-ABNORMALITIES
11. SEX EDUCATION

An Outline of Sexual Morality

Chapter 1: Apologia

I HAVE been impelled to attempt this definition of sexual morality for at least three reasons. The first is that, at this moment particularly, science is emphasizing the large responsibility which sex assumes in our lives. We may think that Freud has overestimated this influence; nevertheless, all psycho-analysis tends to show that the sex-force cannot be wholly repressed and that even with the most passionless individuals sex is the unconscious motive in a large percentage of their activities. It is well therefore that we should have as clear a conception as possible as to the moral rights of this enormous factor in our lives.

Secondly, a handbook of this kind is perhaps the most convenient medium for defining my personal attitude towards this problem. My own views are, of course, unimportant, but it so happens that I have often been asked, in private conversations, to define them. Now to summarize them to the extent which a casual conversation must almost necessarily entail, is difficult; and often, I suspect, I may have given a wholly wrong impression. I am anxious to set that right.

But my chief reason is the chaos of public opinion on this question. One is continually having this fact forced on one. Largely this is the result of transition and reaction. In England, the country to which I shall almost entirely confine myself, we have been enormously affected by that presentation of religion which has been called Puritanism. We have been steeped in the theology of Milton. All forms of religion—Catholic as well as Protestant—have been comparatively infected. When we speak of the "religious attitude" towards any question, we find ourselves irresistibly considering the Puritan attitude.

It is not, I think, unfair to define the influence of Puritanism as a tendency to regard all amusement with disfavour. The original Puritans were notoriously dour in their manner and their dress. It has been said that they attacked the sport of bear-baiting, because it gave pleasure to the onlookers, and not because it was painful to the bears. Sunday, on which the outward observance of religion was necessarily concentrated, became a day of complete abstention from worldly recreation. Puritanism might supply spiritual compensation, but anything which gave pleasure to the senses was essentially evil. Thus art and beauty were banished from religious services and sacred buildings. Not only was the stage an entrance to hell, but a consistent Puritan like Bunyan prayed God to forgive him the sin of having played a game of hockey.

Puritanism had reached its zenith, not of intensity but of universality, by the latter half of the last century. Those of us who are old enough to have been Victorians were brought up on comparative doses of the Puritan medicine. Especially among the middle-classes the history of every English family from the eighties till the War is extraordinarily similar; it consists of a series of emancipations. Our grandparents were almost entirely Puritan in their manner of living, our parents had compromised and extricated themselves to some degree, and our children have become almost wholly free. How many of us realize that up to the seventies it was quite improper for a lady to ride on the top of an omnibus?

In no instance was the effect of Puritanism stronger than on sex. For sex is pre-eminently inspired by a desire for pleasure, whether it be spiritual, emotional, or carnal. On this score alone it would have been marked out as a deadly evil. But there was a further indictment in the Puritan creed. According to the Miltonian interpretation Paradise had been lost on account of the sex impulse; "original sin" was nothing more or less than the sense of sex—the loss of sexual ignorance. Accordingly the whole sex-nature was regarded as evil, and sex generally became a taboo, a closed subject to which no reference could be made. Victorian Puritanism often, indeed, suggests the ostrich burying his head in the sand—the attempt to remedy evil by pretending that it does not exist.

The effect of Puritanism on the Victorian was precisely this conformity of outward behaviour. It assumed that all men and women were innocent, and that, except in marriage, sex played no part in life. It pretended they were innocent, and it made them only respectable. Parents would often refrain, on the plea that innocence must not be disturbed, from teaching their children anything about sex. So impure and evil a subject must not be referred to. Such unpleasant problems as venereal disease must be hidden out of sight, although prostitution and venereal disease continue to flourish. The Victorian, in fact, carried out the Puritan doctrine that all sex is evil, by outwardly pretending that, unless married, he possessed no sexual instinct. Actually he was no more inclined to abstention than any other human generation has been.

Indeed, we do not find any evidence that Puritanism succeeds in carrying its anti-sex theories into practice. In South Wales, for example, where Puritanism has established a particular stronghold, sexual laxity is peculiarly marked.

The reaction from Puritanism, especially in regard to sex, has been precipitated and exaggerated by the Great War. We have therefore in modern society two opposing policies. Among those who have thrown over all "religious" observance and have freed themselves entirely from Puritanism, there seems to be a complete absence of any moral sex-standard. We can appreciate that impasse if we consider the inability of the sex-novel or play to suggest any form of conduct which is immoral. Those who still adhere to organized religion continue to look at sex largely through Puritan spectacles. The "fallen woman" or the convicted clergyman is genuinely regarded as being guilty of the most damning of all offences. The sexual laxity of the neo-Georgian is used as a convincing argument that once the Puritan view is abandoned, complete anarchy is the only alternative. Religious teachers continue to preach what many of them would deny to be Puritan doctrine, but what I hope to prove belongs peculiarly to that aspect of Christianity. And meanwhile the "non-religious world" pronounces the opposite extreme.

It is because I believe both these attitudes to contain error, that I am anxious to contribute the foundation for some principle in the current deadlock.

Chapter 2: Official Attitudes towards Sex

IT will now be convenient to define the chief collective or official attitudes towards sex. In a mere outline such as this handbook professes to be, we may divide these attitudes into three, and label them the popular attitude, the legal or State attitude, and the religious attitude.

With the popular attitude we have already largely dealt. It is still in a transitory, confused state, merging at one end into the old Puritan extreme, and at the other to mere negativism, mere opposition to Puritan asceticism, and without even an attempt to reconstruct a moral standard. This perhaps is an inevitable stage in any transition; but it is none the less unsatisfactory. Man cannot succeed without a standard; and moreover we know intuitively that all things are not morally permissible. If there is purity and beauty and divinity in life, there must be impurity and sin. Will it be considered an exaggeration if I say that it is almost better to have a Puritan standard than none at all? The Roundhead at least was more than a match for the Cavalier because he had a positive inspiration.

But there is one common feature in this chaos of evolving popular opinion. The vulgar mind tends to measure morality by what is usual. The sins which most men commit are regarded as hardly evil; the acts which may not be evil, are regarded as sins if they are peculiar. Thus an occasional lapse from continency on the part of a young man is popularly regarded as not very reprehensible, whereas the perpetrator of some weird act of bestiality would be hounded to prison. The flaw in this estimate is not only that the normal standard varies in race and age, but that there is no single human sex nature; there are infinite varieties. To condemn variety *per se* is, as we shall presently observe, a contradiction of the laws of nature.

The gradual emancipation of society from the taboo on sex in conversation is an undoubted gain. We owe such men as Bernard Shaw a debt of gratitude for the way in which they have forced sex reference into the play, and therefore on public notice. But if this is to result in eliminating sex modesty it is creating evils greater than those which it seeks to remove. I will not here embark upon a consideration of such a theory as that which has been interestingly propounded by Mr. Westermarck, namely that there is a relationship between sexual modesty and the feeling against incest.[1] I will only insist that modesty is natural in all qualities which we regard as sacred.

If we are modest about sex in our conversation to the extent of placing a taboo on sex, and allowing sexual problems to remain unsolved, or in letting our children confuse innocence with ignorance, we are on indefensible ground; indefensible, I think, because our modesty is based on the Puritan doctrine that sex is at heart an unclean thing. I wish especially to defend modesty because sex is so clean. We do not want to vulgarize by public reference our most spiritual experiences, our sense of love, our feeling of exaltation in the presence of what is beautiful and divine. We speak of these things only at more sacred moments, if at all. We must be careful, too, lest in a reaction from taboo we allow science to rob sex of its romantic and divine character. We have carefully to preserve the centre of gravitation between two extremes. We should look askance at a man who collected in a glass bottle, and analysed, his mother's tears.

In this connexion it may be well to call attention to the inconsistency of the male in making the sex-act a subject for humour. Whatever our religious belief, we know that the sex-act is the means of procreation, and is, for this reason alone, a sacred function. It seems inconsistent, therefore, that we should so persistently treat it as a mark for ridicule.

The second general attitude is that of the State, or legislature. Here we find ourselves in the presence of a consistent motive. The State is concerned only with the preservation of the birth-rate; any sex behaviour which defeats this object it regards as immoral and punishable. The State cannot interfere so far with individual privacy as to punish masturbation or artificial means of restraint; but it does go to the extent of punishing "unnatural" acts between husband and wife,[2] and in America, the State has even penalized the activities of the neo-Malthusian propaganda. All sex abnormalities are rigidly punished, whereas the procreation of children outside wedlock is not a legal offence.[3]

This is a consistent attitude, but it suggests one serious flaw. Whatever may have been the case in early days when an increase of population was essential, there can be little doubt that to-day that necessity has diminished. Indeed, without entering into the Malthusian controversy, it is almost impossible to deny that at the moment we are suffering largely from over-population. Consequently, whatever opportunist policy may dictate, we cannot poise our estimate of morality on so shifting a basis as the needs of population. Instinctively we cannot associate morality in anything with the legal attitude. There are many acts even outside the sex sphere which most of us would consider immoral, but which are unpunished by law, and others which are illegal but are not immoral; it is immoral to lie, but unless we lie on oath there is no State offence; it is punishable to ride a bicycle without lights after dark, but we are conscious of no moral delinquency in so doing.

The third attitude is that of religion. We have already discussed the Puritan attitude and the manner in which it has permeated our unconscious religious thought. In the Anglican marriage-service there appears at first sight to be some endorsement of the theory that the sex-act is unclean and is only permitted in marriage as a concession to human weakness.[4] This doctrine owes its derivation to St. Paul, although it is important to notice that St. Paul specially emphasizes that he is not speaking ex-cathedra: "I say therefore to the unmarried and widows it is good for them to remain even as I. But if they cannot contain, let them marry; for it is better to marry than to burn."[5]

These words will probably be used as an argument against the statement that it is a specifically Puritan doctrine to regard the sex-act as unclean. It will be urged that the early Christian Church, as shown by the writings of the Fathers, discouraged marriage and upheld celibacy as the ideal. I hope, in a moment, to differentiate between the Catholic and the Puritan doctrine. But more immediately we will consider what I have broadly defined as the Puritan attitude.

The flaw in the argument that the sex-act is by nature unclean and must be suppressed, even though in marriage it may be legitimized, is that it is the ordained means of procreation. Further than this, we have the inevitable fact to face that the sex-instinct in normal persons is so strong that it can only with great difficulty be suppressed, and then results in an outflow of sex activity in what we usually know as non-sexual channels. Often this suppression will find its vent in mental dislocation and general nervous irritability. But without analysing these complex symptoms, it is sufficient to ask those who admit the control of God, why God created the sex impulse in order that it should be obliterated.

Directly we move away from this strict doctrine to the modified popular expression of it, we find that the position is becoming more intelligible but less logical. It is consistent to regard all sex as evil. But when the average Christian, while denouncing adultery as a sin, insists on copulation in marriage as its consummation, a difficulty arises which must not be ignored. Here, in adultery, is a sin which is so serious in the eyes of Christian men, that it can never be redeemed; the stigma of impurity remains for ever on the offender. Yet this same act, if only committed under the regulation of marriage becomes not merely something permissible, but the essential act of consummation, the divine method of procreation. One can understand how an act, good in itself, can become a sin because it is performed under impermissible circumstances. But it is difficult to conceive of an act changing its integral nature, so that at one moment it is a necessary virtue, and at another the basest vice. It is, for instance, legal for a soldier to kill an enemy in battle, while it is a crime for one civilian to kill another; but the act of killing is *per se* an evil thing, even in the case of a soldier. It never becomes so exalted as is the sex-act in marriage.

The Catholic doctrine, however, while at first sight it appears to be identical with the Puritan, is actually quite distinct.

For one thing there is a difference of attitude towards sin. Puritanism seems to suggest that those who have been "converted" are actually perfect. It insists that they shall keep up this outward appearance, and consequently ensures that their sins must be committed secretly. They are then sufficiently perfect to ascend, after death, direct to Heaven. Catholicism, however, is continually recognizing that man is normally a sinner; the confessional is a public recognition of this fact. Catholicism therefore approaches the question of sex with the expectation that man will sin, that the probability of his fall is so great as to make it unnecessary and undesirable to hide all traces of his sin from public view. The Puritan attitude towards sex is really that of the prude. The Catholic Church is so ready to talk about sex in a decent manner that she provides the confessional as a permanent institution.

When we turn to the Catholic attitude towards sex we are faced indeed with two significant dogmas which make up a position fundamentally distinct from that of Puritanism. The first of these is the doctrine that marriage is a sacrament, and the second that the *esse* of the marriage is the consent of the parties.

The significance of the first is that marriage is not merely a licence whereby an unclean act is permitted as a sop to human weakness. The sex function, as the integral part of marriage, is acknowledged to be an actual objective of divine grace.

The significance of the second doctrine is that wherever two people eligible to give consent, give it, there is the essence of marriage. Few non-Catholics realize that though the Church normally requires the ecclesiastical and civil regulations to be observed, she does not profess to marry the two persons; she merely pronounces a blessing on their marriage. She may make conditions before she will give her blessing or even her witness to the validity of the marriage; but she recognizes that a marriage may be just as valid on a desert island as in a cathedral.[6] And hence she really regards adultery, not as does the Puritan, but as an act which should be sacramental but has been prostituted by the absence of the love-motive, or by becoming promiscuous rather than constant. Sexual union may even itself be of the nature of a marriage, and it is significant that the Church has always insisted on the right of parents subsequently to legitimize children born out of wedlock; it is the English law which has forbidden that privilege.

This is the official Catholic doctrine, however much it has been assimilated to the Puritan conception by the personnel of the Church.

Yet the Church has consistently upheld the celibate life as the higher vocation. She has represented a celibate priesthood as a greater ideal than a married priesthood. She has exalted Our Lady as a Virgin. She has insisted on the Virgin Birth. But she has done this, not because sex is evil, but because celibacy is better. And, as we shall see, religious celibacy is entirely distinct from a condition in which the sex impulse is merely repressed.

Chapter 3: The General Principles of Purity

In attempting to define these principles I have no desire to enter into a controversy of relatives and absolutes. It is sufficient to meet those who deny that there can be any abstract standard of purity by pointing out that we know the direction in which to look for what is good and pure. Just as we know that certain acts are less worthy than others, so we are aware of the general direction of the nobler activities.

The first principle to be observed is that relatively *purity is comparative*. This is a commonplace of all personal estimates. However much we may adhere to the conception of a moral standard, which is abstract and unvarying, we realize that there are also personal standards which vary very much. We do not, for instance, consider a cat to be guilty of murder when she kills a bird; we do not execute her as we execute men who have taken human life. We do not even condemn lions or tigers as homicidal criminals, though we may kill them in self-defence, thus showing that it is not the distinction between taking animal and human life which constitutes the crime; it is the difference between the killers. Nor is it true that we draw a distinction merely between animal and human responsibility, for even in the human kingdom we apply a comparative moral standard; we do not consider a savage who steals or kills as being guilty to the extent which a civilized European would be who performed a similar act. We are in fact constantly applying a comparative standard to the comparative intelligences of individuals, and quite rightly, for all intelligence and moral sense is graded from brute-beast to savage-man and upwards.

We must be careful not to avoid this standard of comparative values in approaching sex morality. So long as we admit that at least there are acts and principles which, taken in the abstract, approach purity more nearly than others, we must not judge all individuals by the same standard. We must not consider a very ordinary, unintelligent, animal-blooded young man as being excessively sinful for having a vivid sex experience; perhaps he is living right up to the level of his imperfect standard. We must not expect people to be more moral than they can be, though it is the duty of Church and religion to educate them to see that there are better standards.

The second principle is simple, but of the deepest importance.

It consists of the proposition that variety and not uniformity is the fundamental rule of nature, or, as Christians would hold, the intention of God.

I cannot recall any distinctive attribute to which this rule does not apply. There are an infinite species of creatures, and infinite tastes and tendencies. Even if we narrow down our field of investigation to one nation or even a single family, we find that each individual is approaching life by different byways, with different prejudices and different temperaments and different conceptions. But throughout history the majority of the normal type has been inclined to flout this divine principle. The Puritans, for example, were a particular type who did not like the gayer life of the world, and preferred a stern evangelical atmosphere. Consequently they regarded those amusements for which they happened to possess no partiality, as evil, and whenever they had the opportunity they suppressed them; they eliminated Christmas and the mince-pie. Equally we can see that if the normal mechanical Teutonic type had said that it was unnatural for men to be artistic and had suppressed the arts, it would have been a disaster for the world. There is not one vocation, but there are many vocations; all types are the design of intention, and are there, not to be suppressed, but to carry out their particular mission.

This again, is equally true of sex, and we must apply the same conclusions towards the many types which we shall presently meet, abnormal as well as normal. The Protestant, for example, really acknowledges a uniform sex-nature only. You will continually hear a Protestant declaring that it is unnatural for a man to be a celibate: this is, of course, pure nonsense. It might be unnatural for a normal sex-nature to remain celibate, just as it would be unnatural for a natural celibate to marry. The Catholic Church has been far wiser. She can offer the Religious Life to the celibate and the Sacrament of Marriage to the non-celibate. There are few types of individual more unintelligent than that which, while it cannot so interfere with personal liberty as to compel marriage, persists in uttering the convention that "every man ought to do his duty to the State." The truism is true; what is wrong is the failure to conceive that there is no uniform duty for every man.

But the third principle is more complex in character, or, rather, in the considerations which it involves.

It consists, really, of a re-affirmation as to the Catholic condemnation of the heresy of Manichæism.

The Puritan and the type he has evolved do radically regard the physical as evil. Protestantism, until it became adulterated by the Catholic movement, eliminated as far as possible, the physical medium in religious worship. Not only doctrinally, but liturgically, in the abandonment of ritual and artistic atmosphere, it attempted to limit religion as far as possible to the spiritual level, and it regarded sacramentalism as evil because sacramentalism involves an outward physical sign. In the same way the average Englishman, who has been inculcated, far more than he realizes, with Calvinist dogma, regards sex as immoral only when it is physical. A man may indulge in sexual emotion and thought, but so long as he suppresses any physical act he is not guilty; if this can be regarded as an exaggeration it is certainly true that popular Protestant theology regards a man as more immoral if he commits the physical sex-act than if he thinks of it. It is strange to note how far this theory has departed from the teaching of Christ, Who declared that "he that lusteth against a woman hath committed adultery against her in his heart."

It is obvious the moment we examine this conception that it is utterly indefensible. If the sex-act is evil[7] because it is physical, then it is equally evil to eat or drink. And if an attempt is made to avoid this difficulty by saying that it is evil to debase love by expressing it in a physical act, or that it is better to love spiritually and non-physically, then it is equally evil to debase artistic inspiration by expressing it with paints on a physical canvas, or better to allow melodies to float in one's mind than to reduce them to the level of a physical composition.

Without entering into a highly involved philosophy and therefore at the risk of apparent dogmatism, I wish now to emphasize that there are certain ascending levels, with which man is concerned. We may confine ourselves to the physical, the emotional, the mental, and the spiritual levels. The physical level is the lowest, in so far as man functions there in common with the animal. He is more active emotionally than the animal. But what distinguishes him chiefly from the animal, and makes him master over all brute-creation, is his activity on the mental level. Physically he is less powerful than the elephant; but because he can function mentally and the elephant can do so hardly at all, he can employ the elephant as a beast of labour. Here then we have a distinct gradation, a gradation which continues to apply within the human kingdom and makes us able to distinguish a civilised man from a savage.

We should therefore apply this principle to sex. Sex activity is more pure or impure according to the level on which it chiefly functions. A man who traffics with prostitutes is not immoral because he is functioning physically, but because he is functioning almost entirely on the physical level. Purity is really sex emphasis on the highest levels. Ideally the physically sex-act should therefore be a mere expression of spiritual, mental, emotional love; it should just happen. The moment one begins to lay the emphasis on the lower levels, the more one becomes correspondingly less pure. Lust, in fact, is the desire only for physical sex experience—the wrong proportion and balance. A man's stage of moral development is to be discovered by the particular level on which he is most active.

We must not avoid the consequence of this principle. We must be prepared to admit as relatively moral, behaviour which popular philosophy might regard as immoral. We must also be prepared to regard as immoral many marriages in which the physical is the chief incentive. The lowest stage of impurity would seem to be reached in cases, whether between man and harlot, or husband and wife, where the physical function is so emphasized that artificial physical aids are invoked in order to excite the physical passions and make them the cause instead of the result of sex emotion and thought.

Chapter 4: Celibacy

IF once the third principle named in the preceding chapter is fully appreciated, we have already laid the foundation of our moral standard. We shall have seen that physical expression is the sacramental form of the invisible and super-physical motive, and that immorality is the shifting of emphasis from higher to lower levels. We shall be in possession of a test by which we may in almost all sex problems determine a comparative virtue or evil of any practice or conduct.

Now this involves the equally fundamental theory that sex is not entirely a physical activity. In the popular conception sex is always confused with physical sex expression. But this conception, I submit, is entirely inaccurate. Even though Freud may be justifiably criticised for straining the word "sex" to include many forces which do not directly tend to incite physical sex activity, he has successfully shown that sex is the motive behind emotions and conduct which would not popularly be termed sexual at all. A musician may, for example, be drawing on his sex-energy in composing or performing musical works; a humanitarian may be sexual in his diffused love of fellow-men and women. We cannot possibly draw a line and say that here sex begins and there it ends. We can only admit that it carries far beyond those particular physical manifestations which we popularly associate with sex.

If we accept the principle of ascending levels of physical, emotional, mental, and spiritual functions, we should expect to find that sex makes its appearance in more than one form. We know, that is to say, that there are, not one, but many emotions and thoughts which are directly sexual, and that there would seem to be every reason why sex, which manifests variety in its physical expression, should be equally various in the realm of the mind. Further than this, we are able to advance the principle that when the emphasis is laid further away from the physical level, the functioning power on that level weakens. Man, as we have already agreed, is a more developed animal than the elephant, because he is active in thought. But he pays the price for this by the inferiority of his physical strength. Similarly, the less mentally equipped are frequently more physically powerful. Like all other rules, there are of course exceptions. But there does seem to be a principle, and a principle that we should logically expect, that the more man functions on what we have described as super-physical levels, the less powerful his strength on the physical level becomes.

Again, we have seen that, morally, the physical level is the lowest. The highest human developments are those which the animal cannot reach. The ordinary physical instincts are not evil, they are simply less evolved. Some of them, like the sense of maternity, are good. But we cannot doubt that man's superiority over the animal lies precisely in his ability to do what the animal cannot do, and that, therefore, the realm of mind is "higher" than the realm of action.

When the Catholic Church therefore presents religious celibacy[8] as being the higher vocation she is enunciating this very principle. She is not suggesting that non-celibacy is an evil state. We do not pretend that the profession of crossing-sweeper is evil because the profession of prime minister is a higher ambition; indeed, it would be probably disastrous to persuade a man who had a natural ability to be a crossing-sweeper to qualify as a prime minister. Relatively, a man performs his moral duty in fulfilling his vocation, for whatever grade it may be designed. The true religious celibate is the extreme exception; no one should attempt such perfection who has not the actual call. The means by which we realize our true vocation is too individual a question to enter upon here.

The whole fault of the puritanic conception of sex is to assume that complete repression should be attempted by all men, and that marriage is solely a concession to failure.[9]

Almost the exact reverse is the truth. The celibate is a rare product. And moreover he is not one in whom sex is repressed; he is essentially a human being in whom the sex-force is sublimated into non-physical channels. This may take the form of extreme religious devotion, in wide humanitarianism, in a love of children or animals, in artistic creation or scientific research. It becomes true celibacy only when the individual instinct is so far diverted towards these energies that desire for physical sex functions becomes eliminated. Nor is it true that such a man is barren; he is procreating, as really as the father, a mental or spiritual progeny.

We cannot emphasize this distinction too strongly. For the vast majority of men the celibate life is not intended, and to some extent, though, as we shall see, not entirely, other rules apply. What indeed we have so carefully to distinguish is the transference of sex from the repression of sex. To transfer the sex-force is a healthy and natural energy, whereas to repress sex is an evil which must always tend to produce unfortunate results.

Chapter 5: Non-Celibacy

WE have now arrived at a point where we can emphasize a further distinction. We must, in fact, differentiate between those emotions and thoughts which are sexual in the sense that they naturally incite physical sex functions, and those which manifest themselves in non-sexual activities. It may be true that the energy which is exercised in the latter way is itself sexual; that does not matter for our immediate purpose. It is sufficient that the force is at work in a non-sexual channel.

Here then we have two entirely different processes. The first is the shifting of the emphasis of the sex-force from body to mind, so that the sex-force ceases to be concentrated in physical sex-acts and begins to be concerned rather with love emotion and sex-thought; the second is the transmutation of the sex-force to non-sexual channels. Both of these processes are necessary in the life of the non-celibate.

The latter process is what happens naturally in the case of the true religious celibate. His development and temperament are such that his sex-nature finds a complete expression, as we have already seen, in such directions as a general love of humanity, an intense spiritual devotion, the worship of art or nature. There is no repression, but a full exercise of the sex activities in a "non-sexual" direction.

The vast majority of men, however, are not so developed, and are not intended to carry out such a life. Yet, for them, too, this process must be to some extent adopted. It is largely a matter of common-sense. The animal exercises no restraint; whenever the sex-impulse arises, it is satisfied—so far, of course, as the opportunity is provided. But as we trace the conduct of the more developed species from savage to civilized man we are conscious of a new element of will-power. The influences which cause this power to come into operation may vary. Religious obligations, considerations of business, social, or intellectual responsibilities, help to intervene. An intelligent man simply cannot afford to give vent to sex proclivities every time they arise; he has other interests which must of necessity at many times of the day have the first claim. Imagine a man who sacrificed a business engagement for some sex gratification! Often in the recent war a man, however strong his sexual emotions, would be forced to cast away all ideas of sex in order to dodge a shell; his mind for continuous periods would be so driven with anxieties and the stress of responsibility that sex would sink into insignificance. This is an extreme instance, but to a lesser degree it is what is happening to everyone who leads a normal life. The more developed the man, the wider his intellectual interests; and it is precisely in this capacity to exercise his will-power that he proves his superiority over the animal.

This process of transmutation is the remedy which must be applied in cases where men find themselves the victims of sexual emotion out of all true proportion, whether in married or unmarried life. Mere repression is useless; it is actually harmful. But the mind must be switched off to dig a thought-passage in other directions, in non-sexual interests. Where there is undue sex obsession there is disease. And this mental transference is the chief cure. Really, this transmutation is a diffusing of the sex-force into a wide general area. The man is no longer concentrating all his sex-energy in love for one particular person; he is beginning sexually to love all humanity. He is finding sexual expression in the "non-sexual" forms of art or nature. He is still in love—but in love with love, rather than with one separate personal fragment of the whole.

But with the ordinary man, there must remain a balance of sexual inclination which cannot entirely be transmuted. Here we encounter the first process, and our problem, particularly in non-married life, becomes acute. Is it possible, and is it healthy, to deny the sex-instincts all satisfaction? Different answers are given by religious advisers and by men of the world, while even in the ranks of the medical profession there is no consensus of opinion.

I suggest that there is only one general principle which can be our guide.

The natural tendency of all sexual thought and emotion is to find its outlet in physical expression of some kind. If a man indulges in sexual thought, it is almost impossible for him to avoid a physical result. He may have recourse to prostitution or he may commit solitary practices. The tendency of Puritan morality is, as we have seen, to regard the physical act as the sin and to avoid the conclusion that the thought is evil; consequently the patient is urged at all cost to refrain from action. Let it be stated, quite frankly, that this attitude is scientifically and morally indefensible. It is the thought rather than the act on which the responsibility should be weighed. I have no hesitation whatever in asserting that it is worse, medically and morally, for the individual to indulge in sexual thought and repress the consequent action, than to commit it. The mere absence of physical conduct is harmful and deplorable if the mind is a seething mass of sexual energy which is being denied all outlet.

The first duty in such cases is, as we have seen, to apply the process of transmuting this sexual thought to non-sexual interests, so far as this can be done. The extent to which this is possible must vary in each individual nature. The comparative balance then remains. And here we must bring into play the moral principle to which I have already referred—namely that the morality of sex is determined by the extent to which love is the motive. Sex inspired by love is moral; sex inspired by any other motive is not. The part which the physical sex-force should alone play is the sacramental expression of pure love; so employed it is a perfect and divine activity. When the love-motive is absent, or is not the dominant incentive, the sex-force becomes comparatively immoral and abused.

This is a general principle which can be rigidly employed. And I do not want to escape from the consequences of this doctrine. It appears to me the one natural, fundamental principle upon which a moral standard can be based. Therefore I am ready to accept the conclusion that there are many marriages which are highly immoral because the sex-act is not an expression of love, but either a mere mechanical duty or the result of a physical and emotional excitement, as distinct from love. On the other hand there are many sex adventures, inspired by love, which do not occur within the matrimonial state. This principle alone must guide us in any moral estimate we draw.

Let us apply this doctrine by taking the simple case of a man and woman who are accused of having committed adultery. We inquire first, whether mutual love was the true motive, whether in fact the act of adultery was an unpremeditated incident which occurred as naturally as the kiss which a child gives to its mother. We draw a clear moral line between the sort of assignation which has for its one object the gratification of physical sensations, or the even lower motive, so far as the prostitute is concerned, of substituting for love the earning of a few shillings. But suppose we are satisfied that the physical act was not the object but the result, and that there was love. We go on to ask how deep was the love, and if a deep love is alleged, we ask why the parties are not married. For it is doubtful whether normal love can be wholly spasmodic. It seems contrary to the very nature of love that a man should love one woman for an hour and then throw her over for someone else. The essence of love tends to completeness and permanence.

But we will imagine that even these conditions are satisfied, and that financial difficulties or parental objections alone prevent the formal marriage. We have also discovered that the two people have loved each other for some time, and that there is not therefore simply a sudden fascination, but a love based on knowledge and matured by experience. We are then left with a technical and not a moral offence. In effect a marriage has taken place; there has been the consent which is the essence of the union. It is only when the Catholic conception of the sacrament of matrimony is abandoned that we find ourselves regarding the ceremony in Church or registry-office as the union, and that therefore a moral offence is committed in the sex-act where no such ceremony has taken place. It is true that the parties would be in honour bound to receive the blessing of the Church. The union is irregular; but it is a true union.

Incidentally, I suggest that this theory may be the basis of the scriptural exception in St. Matthew's gospel made as regards divorce where there has been "fornication," or a pre-marital sex-act—namely that by this act a natural marriage has been consummated, and that the subsequent marriage is therefore invalid.

One might almost draw up a schedule of the tests which should be applied whenever we may happen to be forced to adjudicate as to the morality of any sex-behaviour. For already there have emerged certain definite test-principles. There is the consideration of the standard of the relative degree of intelligence to which the particular individual has developed, and of the fact that there are many types of sex-temperament. On the other hand we see that the direction of absolute morality to which our faces should be set, is the raising of the sex-force to super-physical levels, so that the physical side becomes a mere incident, or is even eliminated altogether. Then we apply the rule that there must be an exercise of restraint and will-power, so that sex obsession is entirely avoided. The extent to which the mind can be diverted from sexual channels must depend on the stage of development which the individual has reached. Lastly, we apply the test of how far love, so deep and pure that it is permanent rather than spasmodic, a monopoly rather than promiscuous, is the motive.

Modern society has gone, I contend, as much astray in drifting to the extreme of considering all things permissible, as has Puritanism in regarding the sex-act outside marriage as in all circumstances a deadly evil. And I can only marvel that this latter attitude is taken up so often in the name of the Christian religion, when its Founder, while declaring that at the last day it would be "more tolerable for Sodom and Gomorrah than for the Scribes and Pharisees," also said to the woman taken in adultery, "Neither do I condemn thee; go thy way, from henceforth sin no more."

Chapter 6: Divorce

In leaving the moorland of general principles for the fields of particular problems it will be convenient to group sex natures under three heads: (1) the normal or hetero-sexual, (2) the invert or homo-sexual, and (3) the neuter or sexless. It is necessary only to add that it will not be possible to deal in more than the merest outline with any of these important questions.

The most prominent of the problems concerned with the normal group is that of divorce. The problem arises because on the one hand there is a sense that marriage ought to be a permanent state, while on the other, there are many human exigences which go to break up particular marriages. Separation, without permission to re-marry, is of course an admitted remedy. But the question then arises whether parties so separated will continue to live as celibates; and as it appears certain that the vast majority will not, we have to ask whether it is better to legalise the fresh unions which are formed, or to permit adultery.

Every modern State has wrestled with this problem, and for the most part ineffectually. Where there is no divorce, as in England before 1857,[10] or among the poorer classes who cannot afford divorce, irregular unions and prostitution undoubtedly flourish. Where a compromise is introduced, the permanence of marriage, and therefore of the home, becomes correspondingly impaired, while there are left a number of unhappy cases for which divorce is not allowed.[11] The English civil law is particularly unhappy in its compromise. It is based on the Protestant interpretation of the passage in St. Matthew already mentioned, namely that divorce is permissible where adultery has occurred, and it goes on to make it easier for the husband to sue for divorce when the wife has committed adultery than for the wife to do so in the reverse circumstances. Hence it places a premium on adultery, and exaggerates its importance as regards other sins. It deliberately incites an unhappy wife to commit adultery in order to obtain relief—she can usually evade the vigilance of the King's Proctor—and it singles out adultery as a worse sin than, let us say, cruelty or habitual drunkenness, for which divorce is not at present obtainable. In fact it is difficult to find any logical or moral defence for the English law as it stands.

Let us first see how far the popular critics of the Catholic doctrine of indissoluble marriage are wrong. They regard marriage as simply a contract, from which it follows that divorce should be obtained by mutual consent, or even on the application of one of the parties. But this ignores, among other things, one vital natural law. Marriage begets parenthood, and between the parents of the same child there is a definite and permanent relationship. No Act of Parliament can make men and women cease to be the parents of their own children. Nor, even in childless marriages, is the sense of permanence an artificial convention which can be abolished by the decree of a court. The deeper the love, the more permanent must its nature tend to be. Love is not a contract; it is a spiritual bond.

It is impossible, I contend, to think of a normally healthy marriage without realizing that both the man and woman naturally enter into it with the assumption that it will be a permanent relationship. The possibility of a family, the break-up of the maiden life—even the furnishing of a home, is evidence of a strong probability in the minds of the parties that the step which is being taken is something more than a temporary contract. Indeed, the marriage is only temporary if unhappiness arises. Men and women marry because they want to enter into as permanent a relationship as possible; they enter into it because, as they say, they wish to "settle down." The natural desire of man is that marriage should be permanent.

A reversion to free love would be more than the undoing of the evolution from animal to man. It would completely change the basis of human society. And in proportion as any divorce law encourages the conception of a temporary contract this dangerous instability of home-life is threatened. Americans sometimes describe their own laws as approaching the "ideal." "The question will soon be," wrote a journalist describing the American "smart set," "who is to be your husband next year?"—or, "Has your last season's wife re-married yet?" This is of course an exaggeration; but it is a warning as to logical developments.

In fact, divorce tends to create itself. Divorce is only applied for where the marriage is unhappy. A fair proportion of unhappy marriages arise because they have been hastily entered into; with due inquiry many of them could have been prevented. But the easier divorce is to obtain, the more incentive will be given to enter into these hasty marriages—the type of union which so often gives rise to divorce.

On the other hand, whatever their cause, there are marriages in which all trace of love has disappeared, and it may fairly be argued that the union is dead. Thus a husband may, in later years, become incurably insane or habitually drunk. There are many unions in which the one party has married in blind infatuation only to discover that the partner is so contemptible a creature as to destroy all vestige of love. Such unions remain marriages in formality only; their pretended existence is a sacrilege, particularly if there are no children and the husband and wife are not therefore co-related as parents.

For all such cases the Catholic Church permits divorce (*a mensa et thoro*)— or separation, as it is known in civil law, without permission to re-marry. The issue, therefore, becomes simply a question as to whether it is right to expect the parties so separated to remain celibate.

In an outline such as this, I suppose that one can only attempt a summary reply to these questions. If, for a moment, we are to exclude the complications of a subsequent love-affair there appears to me to be no reason whatever why any man or woman should not remain celibate during the lifetime of the divorced partner. The *journalese* theory that it is unnatural and unhealthy for people so to remain is simply untrue, so long as the celibacy takes the form of sublimation or transmutation and not repression. The complication of an intense love-romance however, is a serious proposition. Ought two people in love to remain sexually apart simply because one of them is still married to, let us say, an incurable lunatic? In principle there seems to be every reason why they should; no actual physical or mental harm is done to them, provided they have a sufficiently developed will-power to transfer their sex-desire into other channels of activity. The sacrifice will be immense, but it is no more than any man has to make who refrains from marrying his beloved because he is too poor or is suffering from some disease which may affect his children. In this case the sacrifice is offered for the supremely important principle that only God, by the act of death, can undo the vinculum of the original marriage.

But I am equally sure that most people under these or less intense circumstances will not remain celibate.

Therefore, to descend from theory to practice, I see no alternative but to draw a rigid line between civil and religious marriages. The State must make its own arrangements and go its own way. But there should always be a higher type of marriage where the Catholic Church has been invoked for her blessing. And for those who choose to ask for this sacrament, the union should be irrevocable, save by death. The parties will receive that sacrament knowing what a heavy responsibility they are assuming. And it is only right that the Church should be far more particular in refusing to prostitute her sacramental grace on unions which ought not to be consummated. She ought, I conceive, rigidly to inquire into the desirability of the union, and not to give her blessing unless she is satisfied that both parties are giving their consent with as full a knowledge of the facts as is humanly possible. Equally she should refuse her ministrations where she is unconvinced that love is the motive of the marriage. I see no reason why some form of sponsorship should not be demanded.

And I think it may be argued that a consent without a knowledge of the facts is not a valid consent, and that such a union is null. I should welcome a careful extension of the decree of nullity, for that reason.

Chapter 7: Eugenics and Prostitution

THE doctrine that love is the only motive for sex—that physical expression is pure only so far as it is the sacramental accidence of love—leads to important conclusions. There is, for instance, a class of moralist who teach that the sex-act in marriage must only be for the purpose of procreation. It would follow from this that it is immoral for sex intimacies to occur between a man and his wife once she has passed a certain age. In the ideal marriage, so this school of thought affirms, copulation is strictly regulated and occurs only when the moment is favourable for generation.

To this theory I cannot subscribe. It runs counter to the doctrine in which I believe. It Changes the sex-act from an incident or a result to a means or a cause. It is really immoral because it lays emphasis on the physical. This cold-blooded calculation of the times when sex is to be thus physically expressed is the exact opposite of the principle by which love directs and the act merely occurs, with no purpose but to express love physically.

This leads us to a consideration as to how far those practices between man and woman are moral in which procreation cannot result. It is interesting to note that the English law holds that "unnatural" acts between husband and wife are criminal. Although it is true that prosecution cannot occur unless there is an absence of consent, for otherwise there would be no evidence—these acts are apparently regarded as *per se* criminal in nature. And this indeed is a logical position, when we remember the standpoint which the State adopts towards all sex questions.

To this class of conduct artificial preventatives are closely allied. A chaos of opinion rages over this subject, from the neo-malthusian who advocates the practice as a necessity, to the purist who talks of "child-murder." It seems clear that this latter designation is an unwarrantable exaggeration; to prevent the possibility of life coming into existence cannot by any strain of imagination be confused with destroying what is actually alive. On the other hand, the moral test which we are applying to all these problems hardly acquits the practice. It is difficult to think of preventatives without being conscious that premeditation of the physical act is being emphasized, and the ideal of a natural incident almost banished. To prepare for a thing is to insist on its importance. The minds of the two parties must almost necessarily be focussed—though not absolutely necessarily—on the physical sex-act.

There is no doubt however that, apart from ideals, preventatives are a means of averting more serious evils. This is not the place to enter into a detailed consideration of eugenics. We can only face the blatant fact that thousands of degenerate parents continue each year to breed degenerate children. The moral aspect with which alone I am dealing, is that this is a crime against the community; however irresponsible or ignorant the perpetrators, they are helping to burden the State with an altogether undesirable progeny. Now, whether they are allowed to marry or not, there is not the least likelihood that they will desist from sexual intercourse. Therefore, it seems to me an obviously lesser evil to remove all excuse for procreation by placing within reach the artificial means of prevention.

In this, just as in the divorce problem, we have to determine whether it is better to insist on an ideal, which we know the majority will not keep, or to legislate down to the majority. There is no doubt in my own mind that to legislate on an ideal is not only impracticable but dangerous. I may believe, for instance, that it would be a higher ideal to live on vegetables and fruit rather than to slaughter animals and drink their blood. But even so, I should vehemently oppose a law which attempted to impose vegetarianism.

I believe, too, that every moral influence should be brought to bear against marriages where the physical or mental degeneracy[12] of the parents renders the use of preventatives desirable. I wish to emphasize that the ideal towards which we should set our faces is that of fewer but healthier marriages. Both Church and State should, I feel, take pains to assure themselves that these undesirable elements are absent in all unions which they are respectively called upon to solemnize. And I emphasize this because I believe that we are suffering far too much from the popular fallacy and the smug Puritanic doctrine that the cure for all sexual proclivities is for men and women to marry, and that once they marry all things are sexually permissible. It is not only irritating, but it is a fallacy, for men who are comfortably married to declare that there is "really no sex-problem." There is probably as much immorality within the married state as outside it; and far from it being the duty of every man to marry, there are many men whose duty it is not to do so.

Closely allied with eugenics is the problem of venereal disease, and out of this again, arises the problem of prostitution. How far is prostitution tolerable, so that a medical system of registration should be introduced into England? We have seen why prostitution is immoral; it is concerned with the physical side of sex, and with little else. But no thoughtful man could reasonably advocate the suppression of prostitution by law. The result of such a measure, at the present state of national development, would be deplorable, even if it were practicable. People do not become moral because they are frightened to do what they still want to do. It is always a confession of the weakness of religion or moral influences where you have to fall back on the police-force of the State for support. In moral questions, State prosecution seems only to be justifiable where the liberty of individuals, or the welfare of the community, is endangered.

Prostitution[13] as an evil can only be treated by the slow process of moral education. Of that I shall speak later. But it is worth while remembering in this connexion, that the feminist movement must have a beneficial effect, to some extent, on prostitution. Largely, it is an economic problem. If a woman were able to earn a decent wage, it is inconceivable that she should wish to submit herself to every voluptuous patron who happens to come along. Education and economic independence must tend largely to breed dissatisfaction with such a slavish occupation. It will not do so entirely, for a certain percentage of women are prostitutes because they hunger for promiscuous sex intercourse.

That some serious attempt must be made, not merely to alleviate, but to prevent venereal disease, is evident to all who are aware how widespread it has become. And it may therefore be pointed out that it would not be impossible to prosecute the prostitute, suffering from these diseases, without introducing the vexed question of registration and official recognition of prostitution. All unmarried men and women below a certain age could be compelled to submit to periodical medical examination, and if any person was found to have solicited, after having been certified as infected, prosecution would lie. Probably a storm of protest would be aroused against an alleged interference with individual privacy. But the danger of syphilis may necessitate such a law, and after all, no one is being asked to do more than that to which every soldier and sailor has to submit.

We have seen that love, and therefore marriage, naturally contains the sense of permanence. There is also a sense of distaste towards incest, and of the apparently natural evils arising therefrom. No-one will deny that the State and the Catholic Church are scientifically justified in insisting upon some table of prohibited degrees. How far this distaste is essentially natural I do not know. I imagine that a sister who had been separated from her brother since birth, and who did not know that he was her brother, might fall in love with him. But the scientific dangers of such marriages would remain.[14]

The Church of England some years ago found herself immersed in a storm of controversy over the Deceased Wife's Sister Act. To most men her attitude seemed pedantic and unworthy of serious attention. The English Church is unfortunate: her apparently narrow ecclesiasticism was really the result of a liberal policy at the time of the Reformation. During the Middle Ages the Church had extended her prohibited degrees to such an extent that it must have been difficult to know whom one could marry without a dispensation.[15] Only a person more than four degrees removed from the other party was an eligible partner without dispensation, the degrees so being reckoned as to include even second cousins. The English Church swept away these anomalies and concentrated on an irreducible minimum of prohibition up to three degrees (reckoned in direct ascending and descending generation from the common ancestor)—thus sacrificing all regulation against marriage between first cousins, who are four degrees removed.

The real opposition to the ecclesiastical attitude was, however, that any affinity, as distinguished from consanguinity, should be a bar to marriage. The unhappy deceased wife's sister was merely a convenient representative. But this is a controversy which is not sufficiently imminent to engage us in these pages.

Chapter 8: The Homosexual Temperament

WE must now pass from the normal or hetero-sexual to the second-class of sex-temperament. This is the homosexual—that in which the individual's sex attraction is directed towards the same sex. And here it will be necessary to utter a note of warning. The sex instinct lies so deep in human nature that many men are incapable of regarding sex characteristics save through their own temperamental colour. Normal men are frequently found, for instance, of such underdeveloped mental faculties that they start out with an immense sex prejudice against the homosexual. Without being able to consider the question impartially they abhor this variety as an unspeakable evil. It is essential that we should place such critics outside the area of practical investigation. The homosexual tendency may be as evil as they imagine it to be, but we must only arrive at that conclusion as a result of impartial and incontestable reason. And any man who cannot undertake that inquiry is as valueless for our purpose as are his prejudicial opinions; he must simply go back to the nursery.

Let us therefore, as far as is individually possible, attempt to treat this question with an open mind. And accordingly we shall find it most convenient first to consider the various attitudes which have been taken up with regard to this difficult problem.

The legal or State attitude we have already to some extent anticipated. The State looks with suspicious eyes on any influence which tends to sterilize the birth-rate. Accordingly, in England, homosexuality is branded as a crime for which a heavy sentence can be pronounced. It is true that legally this sentence, under the Criminal Amendment Act, can only be inflicted for the physical sex-act itself; but this includes any assault or any behaviour which may be construed as an attempt to lead up to the commission of the act. And, accordingly, any man is legally under suspicion if he is thought to be homosexual, even though no perpetration of the physical offence can be alleged against him. The hideous system of blackmail is thus encouraged by the law. Once a man is understood to be subject to these proclivities, it is assumed that sooner or later he will commit the offence, and he is watched, if not by the over-busy police, by those idle persons who trade upon the legal attitude toward this problem. Any conversation or literature on the subject is suppressed, so far as is possible, by the State, because the physical expression being a crime, all that may become an incentive to the crime is itself criminal.

We have already mentioned the basic fallacy of the legal attitude. It does not follow that because a line of conduct may decrease the birth-rate, it is therefore wrong. Celibacy, as we have seen, may be an actual virtue. But in this particular instance there is a still more serious error. The English law, by branding homosexuality as a crime, assumes that it is a deliberate perversion; for it would be obviously ridiculous to punish a man for doing what he could not help doing. Even the law is not so illogical as to sentence a madman to penal servitude because he insists on being mad. No, the State regards the homosexual as one who has of his own choice assumed this form of sex temperament, in the same way as a man decides to rob or forge a signature. The legal attitude *must* rest on this supposition, for otherwise its policy would be flagrantly unjust. And accordingly we find the law classifying this family of behaviour as "unnatural."

Now, if there is one fact which is clear from an investigation of the problem, it is that this supposition is as false as it is possible for any supposition to be. Let it be granted that a certain number of homosexual offences are committed by persons who are sexually normal in temperament. There remains the whole body of homosexuals, of those, that is to say, in whom the homogenic attraction is as integral a part of their nature as the appreciation of music or the love of colour. Abundant proof of this contention is to hand. There have been thousands of individuals in every age, including the present, who have never heard of homosexuality, [16] have never met other homosexuals, or come into contact with anything approaching homosexual practice; and yet they have been homosexual all their lives. I have known persons who believed that no one else in the world shared their aspirations, and also have suffered tortures because of their supposed isolated abnormality.

The State attitude simply ignores this factor, and accordingly reveals itself as unscientific.

It is true that perhaps by such an agency as psycho-analysis reasons could be found in many of these cases why the individual had developed on inverted sex lines; home repressions, the system of early education, the age of the parents, these or other influences, may have produced a complex which has switched the sex-nature on to a particular path. But these reasons do not necessarily show the result to be artificial; it is our very nature indeed which these influences construct. It is impossible to trace an exact line between the inherent nature and the effect which outside influences have had upon it. We must, and we do in fact, regard the permanent and fundamental traits, however derived, as "natural."

Moreover psycho-analysis definitely indicates that there is a homosexual period through which all individuals inevitably pass.

The State theory that the temperament is "unnatural" cannot therefore be supported on any grounds, except in the cases where it is deliberately assumed by normal persons. In most cases it is natural to the individual's nature, and not "unnatural," but "abnormal."

Once this simple scientific truth is grasped the legal attitude is seen to crumble in all directions. The case for criminal prosecution rests logically on the assumption that unless homosexual practices are rigidly suppressed they will spread. And since their increase would seriously diminish the birth-rate the State is necessarily anxious to avert this danger. But it is an odd perversion which imagines that sober respectable citizens are only restrained from indulging in homosexual vice by the threat of penal servitude! Once the scientific truth is grasped and homosexuality is seen to be, except in a small number of cases, the natural temperament of a small minority, it will be realized that normal persons are not likely to wish to commit unnatural acts, whether there is or there is not a penal law; nor can any Act of Parliament prevent homosexuals from being homosexual.

And in practice this theoretical conclusion is found to hold true. For in the countries, such as France, where the Code Napoléon does not cover these prosecutions, homosexuality is far less rife than in England, or in Germany, where until the Revolution the penal law was rigidly enforced.

It is well that we should face these facts unreservedly, however strong may be our personal antipathy to the practices.

The second attitude may be described generally as that of society. Public opinion must necessarily be too vague to admit of succinct definition. But generally its attitude towards this question may be defined as that of an ordinary man towards a freak; he has no sympathy with freaks and indeed dislikes them—but they are so very rare that he can afford to ignore them.

The problem of the homosexual cannot however be avoided in this way, for the simple reason that the invert forms so comparatively large and permanent a part of the community. It is difficult to attempt an accurate estimate, partly because many homosexuals are so afraid of incurring the odium of public opinion that they successfully disguise their true nature and are unsuspected even by their most intimate friends. But there is a more fundamental difficulty. It appears to be undeniable that a large number of normal people possess to some extent a strain of the homosexual temperament. We have, in fact, as in almost all classifications, not a naturally dividing gulf but a gradually ascending scale. Some individuals may have only 5 per cent. inverted and 95 per cent. hetero-sexual tendencies, while others are only 10 per cent. normal. There are a large and increasing number of persons who are almost equally balanced on either side. These bisexuals often marry happily and at the same time enjoy homogenic experiences.

When we remember that, according to psycho-analysis, everyone about the age of puberty passes through a homosexual stage, it is probably not an exaggeration to state that few people fail to preserve a stratum of this nature, however small the percentage and however deeply such tendencies may be buried in the unconsciousness.

If however we decide to draw an arbitrary distinction and to define persons with less than 30 per cent. inverted nature as normal, persons from 30 to 60 per cent. as bisexual, and the remainder as homosexual, we are left with a considerable number of the last variety. Havelock Ellis has reckoned the percentage of homosexuals among the professional middle classes in England as 5 per cent. and among women as 10 per cent.[17] In any case the popular view that the proportion is so small as to be negligible is quite impossible, and is due to the fact that most men are so unobservant of psychological evidence that their opinion is of little serious value.

However undesirable, then, this species of temperament may be, it cannot be described as unnatural in the sense of artificial or unusual. The third or current scientific attitude does seem at first to avoid these superstitions and to rest on a reasonable basis. This attitude may be described as that of regarding homosexuality as a disease, which should neither be punished nor ignored, but treated. The theory that we all pass through a homosexual period at a comparatively early stage, lends support to this conclusion. The hero-age of boys and girls, it is urged, is almost always directed towards the child's own sex. Therefore it can fairly be argued that where the sex development has been restricted to these lines it denotes some strange dislocation which has prevented natural growth. The fact that in some cases this cause can actually be traced—such as a disappointment in an early love affair with the opposite sex, or to artificial circumstances which have made for celibacy—confirm many students of sex-science in this opinion.

But as if nature deliberately intends to thwart all easily attained explanations, she sets out certain facts, in practice, which entirely invalidate the theory. It is true that many homosexuals, both men and women, portray in general mental efficiency that peculiar want of proportion in some direction which is the inevitable symptom of mental abnormality; the male may be obviously effeminate, or, male or female, eccentric or hysterical. But this is distinctly the exception. So far as my personal experience goes, the majority of homosexuals are indistinguishable from normal men, except by some psychic or intuitional sense, in physical or mental appearance; and I observe that this experience is shared by all those scientists who have written on the subject. The undeniable facts are that among this minority of the race a majority of men have, in all ages and races, held a pre-eminent and honourable position in society, revealing the brilliance of sanity rather than the abnormality of genius. The homosexual has succeeded not only as might have been expected in the arts. It is true that, in general, he possesses certain feminine attributes, such as a gentler and more emotional positivity than the normal. But he has excelled in such masculine paths as soldiering, statesmanship, and engineering. It is almost irritating, where one wishes to find support for the scientific explanation, to turn to history and discover that the homosexual section of the Greeks were magnificent warriors as well as philosophers; that not only Shakespeare, who wrote many of his sonnets to a boy, or Michael Angelo, but Alexander the Great, Charles XII of Sweden, Frederick II of Prussia, and William III of England, had their homosexual tendencies. Indeed, were it permissible to do so, it would be possible to instance some of our most famous generals and politicians of modern times as possessing this unmistakable temperament.

It is well then freely to admit that the scientific theory simply does not square with the full facts of the case.

The fourth attitude is that of religion. The Church's official position is mainly indistinguishable from that of the State, although the atmosphere of the Church has tended largely to be congenial to this development. It is evident that Christianity was influenced in its early days by the appalling condition of vice in Roman society, and it is not to be wondered at that a severe legacy of prejudice has been inherited in the light of this indescribable experience. But this brings us conveniently to a point where we must admit a fallacy underlying almost all considerations of the homogenic sex nature. And unless we are able to dispose of the fallacy in our minds, further investigation is useless.

The fallacy consists of the assumption that homosexuality means only the perpetration of the physical sex-act. In reality this is as untrue as to suppose that the normal man is necessarily a patron of prostitutes. Such a confusion of thought is obviously ludicrous. But not less inaccurate is this prevailing idea regarding the homosexual. Not only is the particular sex-act, popularly associated with this subject, an extremely rare occurence, even as among the physical sex-expressions of this temperament, but probably a vast majority of homosexuals are deliberately celibate. Homosexuality is a romantic cult rather than a physical vice. Nine-tenths of its energy is directed purely in the realm of ideals. The old misconception of sex as a rather disreputable physical function again dogs our steps. But sex is almost entirely emotional; sex-love, and especially homosexual love, is not lust. Its desire is romantic and idealistic, and when physical incidents occur, they are usually the unintentional outlets of the purely emotional passion.

The literature of homosexuality is almost entirely romantic, and small though it is forced to be, in quality and ideal its average must rank as extraordinarily noble.

It is noticeable, indeed, that in a large proportion of the unpleasant cases which are tried in police-courts, the offenders are admittedly normal men who have deliberately perpetrated homosexual acts for various causes, such as a neurotic desire for novelty, or the desire to avoid disease. There are also the considerable class of perverted normals whose deviation from their natural path as the result of some such influence as heterosexual disappointment or repression, has been so emphasized as to render their perversion distinct from natural developments, and who refuse, or are unable, to deny themselves physical gratification.

If we dissociate the true homosexual from this class, and concentrate our attention only on the "celibate" species of such attachments, it is evident that we are in the presence, not merely of something which is not criminal, but of an ideal which is sacred in character. Pure love, especially so intense a love as the homogenic attachment, is not profane but divine. And though the Church may be unable to recognize it by her sacramental benediction, because, unlike marriage, it cannot effect physical procreation, she possesses such Biblical precedents as the story of David and Jonathan—an episode which is obviously homosexual in the sense that it describes not a platonic companionship but a romantic passion.

In the social sphere also, the place of this aspect of homosexuality is obvious. The homosexual must, and does in fact, exist in the most honoured offices of the community. Indeed, it is no exaggeration to declare that few men can be successful in educational or philanthropic work unless they have some homogenic temperament in their nature. Without this they may compel discipline but they are powerless to attract sympathetic co-operation. The testimony in favour of this assertion is overwhelming.

But when we admit that sex tends to find a physical expression, and we come therefore face to face with the physical problem, the difficulty I admit to be considerable. And I can only re-emphasize that this feature is numerically and potentially the least important, but that there can be no religious countenance for any physical sex-act outside the sacrament of matrimony.

Rape, and seduction without consent, are obviously evils calling for legal prosecution, as being an infringement of personal liberty. And in this connexion it must be remembered that homosexual practices tend to seduction, inasmuch as the attraction is frequently towards those who have not attained intellectual manhood. For the rest, I am inclined only to re-affirm the general principle which I have already attempted to define—namely, that sex becomes a sin where the main objective becomes the physical gratification. Once the proportion is weighed on the side of physical expression, love is prostituted. The purity of true love is known by the fact that its face is turned not to mere physical functions, but beyond the emotional and even mental, to the spiritual ideal. Indeed, a lover, whatever his temperament happens to be, loves even if his beloved is removed from all physical reach. That is the test.

I do not look for salvation to the arms of mere criminal legislation. This seems to me to be almost powerless as a moral force, and indeed, to encourage the hideous apparatus of blackmail.[18] Gradual and unsensational as it may be, I believe that morals can only be improved by educational and religious influences.

And so far as theoretical solutions are concerned I believe that Mr. Edward Carpenter[19] comes nearest to the truth. Nature is deliberate in creating not uniformity but variety, and I doubt if the world would continue if there were only normal men in it. The homosexual has his place, within restrictions, as has the celibate or the sexless type. The real truth, I feel to be, is that few men are wholly masculine or women feminine, and that somewhere, in comparative degrees, homosexuality is in us all. It may become so excessive as to be a disease, or so feeble as to create that unæsthetic, bourgeoise type, which is an unpleasant symptom of super-normality.

We enter the realm of pure conjecture if we attempt to inquire the purpose for which this type has been deliberately created. And I can only record my own entirely unproveable, but definite opinion, that the human race, in the far ages ahead, will return, by a spiral process, to the bisexual species from which I believe it has come. If this is so, the homosexual is apparently a prototype, a preliminary attempt of nature to combine both sex-natures in one individual. And with all his present imperfections, I believe that there are evidences which go strongly to support this conjecture.

Chapter 9: The Sexless Class

THERE is little that need be written on this subject, not because it is devoid of interest, but because it raises no vital sex problem.

The number of sexless people is small, though apparently increasing. It may be questioned whether there are any really sexless people—individuals, i.e. whose sex-nature is non-existent. Probably in most of these cases sex, for some reason or other, is there, dormant but positive. But it is convenient so to classify those in whom, for some reason, the sex-force has never yet been stirred.

It must be remembered that this class is quite distinct from the religious celibate. The celibate has all the sexual ardour for his religious or humanitarian devotion. The sexless man or woman is cold, intellectually aloof, and generally critical.

There are only two considerations calling for remarks on this interesting psychological problem. The first is that we must not allow the great body of normal opinion to label such people as unnatural, and as having no part to play in the community. They have, on the contrary, an important rôle. Their intellectual ability is in itself a great asset, particularly in abstract and critical directions. And in all sex questions they should, and frequently have, an impartial outlook, for the very reason that they can view sex from a detached standpoint.

But, conversely—and this is the second consideration—they possess the immoral tendency of regarding sex with abhorrence, especially when they confuse sex with mere physical expression. In extreme cases the sexless individual has been known even to faint or exhibit symptoms of nausea at the chance touch of a woman. This is obviously to magnify the physical side out of all clean proportion. And probably such cases show themselves to be the result of artificial repression and consequent complex. It may be argued from this that all deviations from the normal are the results of repression. But, as we have seen, the difference between natural and unnatural is comparative, and most of our nature is built up, in the first instance, by early exterior influences.

Chapter 10: Super-Abnormalities

UNDER this head I have included a number of characteristics, which have no connective bearing upon one another. It seemed the most convenient classification.

Perhaps it will be best to take as the first example a sex tendency which can hardly be described as super-abnormal, for among single men, and especially among boys, it is extremely common.

Auto-eroticism in the form of self-abuse is not an easy problem to tackle. The usual policy adopted towards boys is most immoral. Well-meaning but hopelessly vicious purists, write terrifying pamphlets or deliver lectures in which they declare that this practice will inevitably lead to lunacy, paralysis or even death. The result is that the boy is scared into an ineffectual attempt at repression, which, so far as it is successful, sets the sex-impulse at work into morose channels and makes him a liar or a thief. Or he may be impelled to inquire for himself. He finds that, so long as self-abuse occurs infrequently, it does not bring about these dire evils, and accordingly he assumes that all moral doctrine is hypocrisy and often falls into the opposite extreme of constant self-abuse, with the result that actual physical and mental deterioration sets in.

What is really the truth?

The first consideration is that frequent and unregulated abuse does cause physical harm. The margin of frequency which will escape this harm varies with the individual. But, with growing boys, the practice is perhaps more dangerous than after physical maturity. The whole reserve of the physical constitution appears to be needed while the body is developing.

The difficulty of this problem is its complications. There are several entirely conflicting influences which must be weighed one against the other.

We have seen the physical danger, and, since morality must not be founded on a lie, we must freely admit that the physical danger may be eliminated by limiting the frequency of the practice. It may then be physically harmless. There remain, however, at least two causes which make for a misuse of the sex-force, that is—for immorality. The first is that it is usually the result of mental weakness, sheer inability to overcome the inclination. The mind, the will, *must* be supreme in its own house. Until that is done little else matters. And it comes, therefore, to this, so far as this particular consideration is concerned, that it is better for a man deliberately to regulate himself by programme to certain times, than to keep up an ineffectual struggle, or to obey whenever the inclination arises.

For, in both these cases, remorse follows. And this is as great an evil as the failure of will; indeed, it *is* failure of will. Remorse is not penitence. It is useless thereby to regret what has been done. A man must simply own to himself that he has failed, make a resolution to be stronger next time, and then sweep the recollection from his mind, switching off on to other mental channels.

The second influence which makes for impurity is that by this practice the sex-force becomes literally selfish. Now, sex is fundamentally a movement towards union through love, whether it be physical or super-physical. This practice is merely a vicious circle, in which the love element, save in the perverted form of narcissism, is absent. Accordingly, there must, almost always, be evil mental results from this abuse. And, once again, we see that the real evil is not in the physical act but in the realm of thought, whether the act occurs or not.

On the other hand, we must not become such abstract moralists as to deny that in many individuals the sex-force is so strong as to press almost irresistibly towards physical expression. Even dreams, which are the normal outlet, may not be sufficient. A man who for some reason, cannot marry, will therefore argue that his only alternative is recourse to prostitution, and that self-abuse, so long as it is regulated, is morally preferable. One remedy is, as we have already seen, the transfer of the sex-force to higher channels, so that all the glow and energy of sex is energized in devotion to a group of persons, or to a religious or humanitarian ideal in concrete labour. For sex is primarily creative, and if it is not creating physical children it may have, and should have, a spiritual progeny—as in art and literature.

The truth is that each individual case must be treated according to its particular state of development. General rules in this instance are particularly dangerous. We can only repeat that the repression is worse than commission, that a seething mass of sexual thought is worse when it has no physical outlet; that the ideal, when there may be no legitimate outlet—and, indeed, to some extent, in all cases—is to find an emotional outlet, to dig thought and emotional channels along which the sex-force may flow, but the physical expression of which is, in the ordinary sense of the term, non-sexual.[20]

And this is quite possible.

II

Attraction towards young children is frequently, perhaps almost entirely, sexual. A symptom of this temperament is that romantic attachments are formed towards either sex, because, before puberty, the child is bisexual or sexless. This must essentially be a cult; it is a clean and noble cult, but the penalty of its high standard is that here all physical sex expression must be denied except in the lesser form of embrace.

Here, indeed, the prosecution of the law against sex-acts is justified. For, not only is the child incapable of giving valid consent, but the commission of the sex-act is physically and morally injurious. It is physically injurious beyond all doubt at a young age, and it is morally injurious, because it introduces sex to an age of development when the consciousness of sex should not have appeared above the horizon. The inevitable result is that if sex-acts take place the child eventually ages rapidly, as can be seen among the child-mothers of India. Maturity is induced far before its time.

The sex consciousness, as distinct from the unconsciousness, can be awakened in the earliest years of childhood. The young boy or girl often shows an extraordinarily intuitive perception that there is a sexual design behind even the apparently harmless overtures. And this is why this cult is particularly dangerous. The lover, in fact, must not only entirely eliminate the morally criminal sex inclinations, but he must take care not to become so sentimental and romantic as really to suggest sex to the child's unconsciousness. It is difficult to draw the line as to what is a lawful and what is an unlawful expression of this sex-temperament. One can only say that the remedy is not to concentrate love on one child, but on children generally. The child must not be treated as an adult; there must be no manifestations of jealousy, or insistence on a return of love expression. The embrace of children must be natural but not too ardent. In fact, the lover must diffuse his love and romp with children as a class rather than allow himself to appear emotional over one individual.

Many unthinking people will at once regard this temperament as impure when they have been convinced that scientifically it is sexual. But this is only because they cannot understand that sex is a clean thing and that the physical side of it is an occasional and by no means an inevitable incident. The cult of child-love is in fact one of the purest and noblest of sex-expressions. But it is a difficult path, and he who treads it must beware of many pitfalls.

Again, I quite deny that it is due to thwarted paternal instinct. I believe it to be as natural a variety as any other of the sex-temperaments. We have suffered too long from the superstition that sex is a uniformity of type.

III

Then there is that strange form of sex-expression known as bestiality.

To most of us the connexion between man and beast in sex is so revolting that there is a great danger of our prejudice running away with us.

I believe that prejudice against what seems to me so debased a vice, is justifiable. But I am equally sure that to punish such offences by criminal law has no shred of justification, except when the act is done in public so as to be openly indecent. No physical or moral harm can be done to the animal. And were it not tragic, the idea of sentencing the offenders to penal servitude would be itself a travesty.

The practice, which is not so uncommon as many people imagine, is not so much immoral as unnatural. I mean that this can hardly ever be a variety of sex-temperament. Although the love of women for pet dogs is probably a form of perverted sex-outlet, it seems impossible to discover here any actual love going out towards animals rather than to humans. Therefore, the act is almost always due to a desire for mere physical expression, when this happens to have been chosen as the most convenient.

The true remedy, therefore, can only be to take the individual and educate him. He must be shown that it is immoral for man to devolve back to the animal level. He is superior to the beast. He must be reminded that sex must be a result of love, and that sex-love between man and animal would only be possible if it were moral for man to cease to reason, to go down on all fours, and to eat and drink and live like an animal. Even the most primitive man would not wish to do that. And if he feels any sense of abhorrence at such a proposal, then he must learn to extend his abhorrence to any attempt at a similar equality in sex.

IV

The strange and almost endless forms of sex-association need not be considered, since they have no moral problem of their own. The man whose sex-force is stirred into energy by the sight of some inanimate physical object is obviously the victim of a sex-repression. And such diseases must be treated as any other repressions should be. These general considerations must suffice here for all forms of sex perversions, such as sadism and its converse. And it is not difficult to distinguish between the unnaturalness of such practices and the natural character of the main sex-types which we have already mentioned.

Chapter XI: Sex Education

It is becoming evident to all students of the sex-problem that the remedy for many of the difficulties arising therefrom is a wholesome and efficient sex-education.

In many cases the parents are not the persons most fitted to give this education. They may not possess the art of imparting knowledge, and often there is a certain reticence between parent and child, which when present creates a bar to the proper handling of this question. The child goes to school to learn, and the school must take its share of this responsibility. Where this is not done the effect is deplorable. In the preparatory school sex has hardly appeared. But in any school where there are older boys or girls, and where sex-education is not given, knowledge is rapidly obtained. Officially sex is ignored until, on rare occasions, it is detected. Severe punishment is then meted out, and perhaps the offender is even expelled, although the school is really penalizing the results of its own system.

It is unnecessary to labour the apology that the absence of sex-education ensures innocence. In no school is this the case. If it were, with growing boys and girls, it would be unnatural. Sex-instinct is bound to grow as the physical body grows, and to ignore this fact is to create the conception that sex-instinct is immoral. We then obtain the usual attitude adopted in public schools—that sex is to be indulged behind closed doors and sex literature sniggered at in dark corners. The boy grows up with a totally unclean view of sex. He becomes either an intolerable prude, or else he approaches sex-experience with an entirely twisted conception of sex-morality. One is continually meeting instances of this perverted imagination. Not only boys, but men, will regard an outspoken book on sex, perhaps written with the purest of motives, as "hot stuff," something to be greedily devoured when the eye of respectable authority is conveniently removed. Recently, a man was told that a certain clergyman was a member of a group of students studying sex-psychology. He expressed the opinion, with a knowing leer, that "some parsons are not such fools after all."

These crude examples of the result of driving sex into a dark corner exactly represent what one is up against in school, and in the world, when one begins to deal with sex openly and cleanly as a natural and non-repressible instinct. Really these people are a type of prude, much as they would resent this classification, for they persist in regarding sex as something which is rather naughty. They even imagine that to take away from it the cloak of unnaturalness with which they have surrounded it is to rob it of all its attraction. This is ridiculously untrue. Sex is attractive because it is romantic, and, so long as one does not go to the opposite extreme of regarding it merely through the musty glasses of scientific classification, it becomes no less attractive when it is open and natural, and ceases to be the cause of giggling asides.

Before any moral sense in the sex-problem can be established there must be a fundamental cleaning of this cess-pool, this strange medley of official silence, unnatural repression, and unclean secretiveness. The main road to a moral sense is sex-education. And it is necessary, therefore, to conclude this outline of principles by suggesting some conditions which should govern such instruction.

It is obvious that sex-education must be advanced on the process of a sliding scale. Before puberty sex should not appear on the horizon of the child's consciousness. The precocious child must of course be specially dealt with, but usually the first lessons in sex should commence with the period of mental puberty. Before that time the small child jokes only about the normal excretory functions, and this can be adjusted by emphasizing the unmanly and unnecessary character of such forms of humour. A child has usually an exaggerated impression of the value of the adult standard, an impression which it must be confessed is too often subject to subsequent disillusionment. While it remains, however, it can be used, and it can be pointed out that "grown-ups" do not consider the excretory system has any more claim to ridicule than the process of digestion or sleep. Vulgarity and coarseness are not symptoms even of immoral sexuality.

The problem commences, then, with puberty. And here a warning should be uttered against that school of reformers which tends to the view that sex can be regarded as naturally and as publicly as natural history or chemistry. This attitude ignores the fact that there is such a quality as sexual appetite. And consequently, sex education should be rather a matter for individuals than for public instruction. We have remarked that the parent may not infrequently be an unfortunate educator. But where these objections do not arise, the home is an admirable atmosphere for sensible teaching. The Catholic Church possesses the invaluable medium of the Confessional, and where the Confessor can give sound sex instruction no better opportunity can be imagined. There remains the school, but even here better work will be done in the study than the classroom.

The immediate problem in the early post-puberty age is the tendency towards solitary practices. It must be recognized that this is usual with all children, and that there is no evidence to show that, save in extreme exceptions, physical harm results. All attempt at *alarmist prudism* must be abandoned. Sane instruction will tend rather to emphasize that sex abuse is due to a weakness of will-power, and that man is most manly, i.e. most removed from the animal, in the exercise of will-power. All education should contain that subject which is at present consistently ignored, namely, the art of thought-control. The child will be interested to follow certain simple rules of mental exercise, and where this is followed the liability to indulge in sex-acts diminishes. It is this element which must be emphasized, the fact, that is, that solitary practices are usually the result of an inability to exercise the will and control the mind.

At a slightly later period, the public-school age, there emerges the tendency, in addition to onanism, for promiscuous practices, usually of a homogenic nature. A further stage of sex-education must now be opened out, namely the principle that physical sex expression must be the expression only of love. The problem now becomes necessarily more acute, but there is this element which tends to lessen the difficulties of the instructor's task. The individual is always interested about himself; he is naturally egotistical. The youth will gladly listen to what can be told him of his own nature. He must be shown the immense superiority of mind both over the emotional and physical natures. This may involve a slight dethronement of the public school appreciation of sport. So long as it is slight such a dethronement will be a reform in itself. The boy in his middle teens must be taught that man is greater in his mental than in his physical activity; he must be reminded that he is inferior to many animals on the physical level. The application of this doctrine to sex is that sex-expression for the purpose of physical curiosity or excitement is a denial of the monopoly of love, which belongs to the emotional and mental capacities.

The young man and the girl, who has left school, will be ready to receive the whole standard of sex-morality as has been outlined in this manual. The chief trouble now becomes over-sentimentality, the tendency to develop emotionally at the expense of the mind. And it becomes, therefore, essential to remind the pupil that where there are continual passing and promiscuous sexual or love affairs, the mind is being shut out from its natural functions. To be attracted sexually towards any pretty girl, to develop sexual relations with different women from week to week, is simply a form of mental unbalance. The emotions are in the saddle. For directly the mind begins to operate there is introduced the element of permanency and constancy. The deepest and most real pleasures only begin in the realm of mentality. The man who hears music only to beat time or remember a catchy tune is shut out of the immense joy of the intellectual love of music. So the young man who lives in a fever of hot-house sexuality, of absorbing intrigues in the dance-room, or the morbid atmosphere of the street corner, is shut out of all the exquisite joys of love. He does not know this, any more than the irreligious man knows what he loses through an absence of the spiritual sense. But he must be told.

The basic principle of sex values is that sex is immoral so far as the physical side outweighs in proportion the emotional and mental—so far indeed, as the act becomes the motive and not the incident. Sex may be dedicated only to love; divorced from love, it is an abuse. There can be no exceptions to this rule, and we can only clarify our ideas as to what is and what is not love. Perhaps this maxim, which we learn by gradual experience, will help us. Sex passion quickly burns itself out. The pleasures derived from passion will be of a purely temporary nature, without the satisfaction which alone comes from permanence. All physical things are less permanent than the mental. There is no joy, no divine nature in sex, save where from the ashes of passion rises the phœnix of the "sexual" but the super-passionate attachment. And this permanent possession can only come, whether in marriage or outside, where the mind, healthily developed and exercised, is taking its true place in the expression of pure love.

Printed in Great Britain by Hazell, Watson & Viney, Ld., London and Aylesbury.

Footnotes:

[1] *The Origin of Sexual Modesty*, by Edward Westermarck.

[2] *Vide* R. V. Jellyman (1838) 8 C and P, 604.

[3] Until recently incest was not a civil offence.

[4] The second object of marriage is declared to be "a remedy against sin...; that such persons as have not the gift of continency marry and keep themselves undefiled members of Christ's body."

[5] 1 Cor. vii. 8, 9. "Burn" means sex-obsession as mentioned on page 38.

[6] "Where the decree Tametsi of the Council of Trent has not been proclaimed, marriage is constituted by mere consent freely exchanged between persons who are by natural and canonical law competent and able to intermarry."—Geary's *Marriage and Family Relations*. (Now altered by *Ne temere*-decree, but the principle remains.)

[7] We have already commented on the strange inconsistency of regarding the sex-act as evil *per se* outside marriage, and as a virtue in marriage.

[8] I am using "celibacy" to imply complete physical chastity.

[9] With the curious inconsistency, already referred to, that in marriage non-celibacy is a virtue.

[10] Except by Act of Parliament.

[11] The Majority Report of the Divorce Commission is a good instance of the unnecessary hardship which results from half-hearted proposals of this

kind. Divorce is to be allowed, for example, after desertion for three years; why not for two? Or again, the wife of an incurable drunkard is to be free to obtain divorce, while the unhappy wife of a man who suffers from violent fits of intermittent drunkenness is to be denied this relief.

[12] I refrain from adding "economic" reasons, for I believe that the State should remove, as far as possible, all such obstacles against healthy parents begetting children.

[13] Procuration for the purpose of prostitution is of course an entirely different matter.

[14] No actual physical harm need result from an incestuous union. The only effect which seems to be caused is that the characteristics to be hereditarily transmitted are doubled. Thus with only a small grain of insanity in a family the chances of aggravated insanity appearing in the offspring of a brother and sister would be considerable.

[15] Spiritual affinity was a bar, so that not only could not godparents marry each other, but there could be no valid unions between a godparent and the child's father or mother. (Geary's *Marriage and Family Relations*.)

[16] Some apology must be made for the use of this hybrid term. The unwarrantable confusion of Greek and Latin terminology must, however, be laid at the door of popular use.

[17] *Psychology of Sex*; Vol. *Sexual Inversion*. Dr. Hirschfeld in his *Statistischen Vatersuchunge über den Prozentensetz der Homosexuellen*, considers that out of 100,000 inhabitants, 94,600 on the average are sexually normal, 1,500 exclusively homosexual, and 3,900 bisexual.

[18] The existence of this danger was admitted in a debate in the House of Lords on August 15, 1921, on The Criminal Law Amendment Bill. The Earl of Malmesbury, speaking on a proposal to apply criminal prosecution to homosexual offences among women, declared that "the opportunity for blackmail will be vastly and enormously increased." Other speakers concurred in this view, and it was partly on this ground that the proposal was thrown out.

www.ingramcontent.com/pod-product-compliance
Lightning Source LLC
Chambersburg PA
CBHW080212040426
42333CB00043B/2615